Who Killed Robert Kennedy?

Philip Melanson

edited by
Sandy Niemann

Odonian Press
Berkeley, California

Additional copies of this book and others in the Real Story series are available for $5 + $2 shipping per *order* (not per book) from Odonian Press, Box 7776, Berkeley CA 94707. To order by credit card, or for information on quantity discounts, please call us at 800 REAL STORY, or 510 524 4000. Distribution to book stores and book wholesalers is through Publishers Group West, Box 8843, Emeryville CA 94662, 510 658 3453 (toll-free: 800 788 3123).

Final editing: Arthur Naiman
Inside design: Karen Faria, Arthur Naiman
Page and cover layout; production coordination: Karen Faria
Basic cover design: Studio Silicon
Cover photo: American Stock Photography
Index: Steve Rath   *Series editor: Arthur Naiman*
Series coordinator: Susan McCallister
Printing: Michelle Selby, Jim Puzey /
    Consolidated Printers, Berkeley, California

Odonian Press gets its name from Ursula Le Guin's wonderful novel *The Dispossessed* (though we have no connection with Ms. Le Guin or any of her publishers). The last story in her collection *The Wind's Twelve Quarters* also features the Odonians.

Odonian Press donates at least 10% (last year it was 36%) of its aftertax income to organizations working for social justice.

Melanson, Philip H.
    Who killed Robert Kennedy? / Philip Melanson ; edited by Sandy Niemann
        p. cm.
    Includes bibliographical references (p.) and index.
    ISBN 1-878825-12-7 (paper) : $5.00
    1. Kennedy, Robert F., 1925–1968—Assassination I. Niemann, Sandy. II. Title.
E840.8.K4M46 1993
364.1'524—dc20   93–15398
                                                           CIP

Printed in the United States of America   First printing, May 1993

Contents

Introduction

Robert F. Kennedy was shot down just after midnight on June 5, 1968, minutes after proclaiming victory in the California Democratic presidential primary. His assassination had an enormous effect on the course of American politics. The country lost a prominent critic of the Vietnam war and a committed champion of civil rights; the Democratic party lost its strongest presidential contender, enabling Republican candidate Richard Nixon to win the November election.

More than four-fifths of all Americans are convinced that they haven't been told the truth about President John Kennedy's assassination. Far fewer are aware that the investigation into Robert Kennedy's death was just as flawed and corrupt.

Chapter 1

Murder in Los Angeles

Bobby Kennedy (as he was almost always called) hadn't planned to run for the democratic nomination in 1968. Many of his closest political advisors encouraged him to wait until 1972, when he had a better chance of winning. In 1968, Kennedy would be facing an incumbent president, Lyndon Johnson, who was still popular in the polls—despite growing protest against his escalation of the Vietnam War.

But then Eugene McCarthy, the other democratic presidential contender, captured 42% of the vote in the March 12 New Hampshire primary. That meant Johnson was vulnerable—and that Kennedy had a chance to win.

Kennedy's entry into the race on March 16 angered Johnson and McCarthy supporters alike. But Kennedy was convinced that if Johnson won, there'd be "more war, more troops [and] more killing"—and less money for the domestic programs he'd so vigorously supported as Senator. McCarthy opposed the war, but Kennedy wasn't convinced he could win the presidency, even if he captured the nomination.

By the June 4 California primary, Johnson had dropped out of the race and

Hubert Humphrey, his vice-president, had announced his own candidacy. Kennedy had won important victories in the Indiana, District of Columbia and Nebraska primaries, but the nomination was still far from secure. California would be a key test—whoever captured that state's 174 convention delegates would have the best chance of becoming the party's presidential candidate.

Early California returns showed McCarthy ahead. But then Kennedy pulled into the lead, and by late evening it was clear he'd taken the state. To celebrate the victory and to hear Kennedy speak, a beyond-capacity crowd of over 1800 supporters began to gather at the Ambassador Hotel in Los Angeles.

The assassination

Tired but jubilant, Robert Kennedy stepped to the podium in the hotel ballroom and stood looking out over the sea of straw hats, balloons and smiling faces. He addressed the crowd with the same message of hope that had characterized his campaign. Lamenting the "division, the violence [and] the disenchantment" within America, he expressed confidence that "we can start to work together. We are a great country, an unselfish country and a compassionate country. I intend to make that my basis for running."

When the applause died down, Kennedy stepped off the podium and started to move toward the crowd. But someone in his party steered him in the opposite direction, toward the backstage exit. Earlier that day, hotel personnel (at the request of Kennedy's aides) had decided to take the Senator on a back route through the hotel's pantry area, to keep him away from the frenzied crowd.

Hotel maître d' Karl Uecker led Kennedy and more than a dozen members of his entourage into a cramped corridor. Even there the crowd couldn't be completely avoided; dozens of busboys, waiters and campaign workers waited, hoping to get a close-up view. Kennedy smiled, nodded and stopped for an occasional handshake as he moved down the corridor and into the pantry.

It was about 12:15 am. Uecker was still slightly ahead of the Senator and to his right. Uniformed security guard Thane Cesar walked slightly behind, also on Kennedy's right. (In 1968, presidential candidates weren't given secret service protection, so the hotel had hired eight private security guards. Kennedy had requested that the guards keep their distance, so he wouldn't be surrounded by uniformed personnel.)

A young, dark-haired man began to approach Kennedy from the front. He was smiling, and bystanders thought he wanted to shake the Senator's hand. But the smile was betrayed by his words:

"Kennedy, you son of a bitch!"

High school student Lisa Urso saw the young man raise the gun and begin to shoot. "I saw the flash [from the gun] and then I saw the Senator....He went forward, then moved backward...grabbed his head and fell backward." It was a "jerking motion"—forward about a foot, then backward onto the floor, limbs awkwardly spread-eagled. A widening pool of blood immediately formed near his right ear.

Uecker heard two shots go off very near his face; he grabbed the assailant's right arm and forced it down on the top of a nearby steam table. "The shooting stopped for just a moment," Uecker later testified, but then "I felt him shooting [again]." Uecker was joined by ex-football player Roosevelt Grier, Olympic champion Rafer Johnson and several others, who attempted to wrestle the weapon from the young man's hand. The struggle was successful but not before the gun was emptied, wounding five other people besides Kennedy.

Busboy Juan Romero knelt and cradled Kennedy's head in his right hand. "Come on, Mr. Kennedy. You can make it."

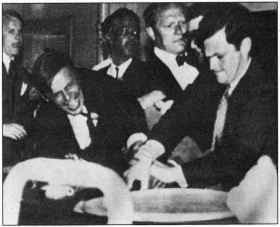

AARC, Washington

The struggle to disarm Sirhan (barely visible in the center). His gun hand is being slammed against the steam table.

Kennedy's lips moved: "Is Paul all right? [Paul Schrade was a labor coordinator for the California campaign and a friend of Kennedy's who'd been walking behind him.] Is everybody all right?"

A young man gave rosary beads to Romero who wrapped them in the Senator's left hand; Kennedy clutched them to his chest. Then Ethel Kennedy, the Senator's wife, and Stanley Abo, a doctor in the ballroom crowd, pushed their way up to Kennedy's side. Ethel knelt over her husband, and Abo took the Senator's pulse. It was slow; suspecting that cranial pressure might be the cause, the doctor probed the head wound with his finger to make it bleed.

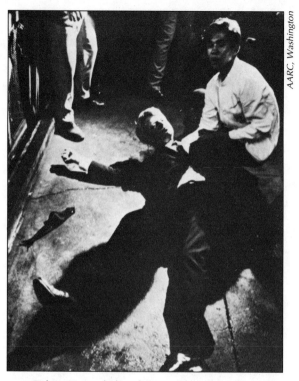

Robert Kennedy lies dying on the pantry floor.

Someone called an ambulance and the Senator was taken to Good Samaritan Hospital. There a team of six surgeons labored to remove the bullet lodged in his brain. But his injuries were too severe. At 1:44 pm the next day, Robert F. Kennedy was pronounced dead.

An open-and-shut case

In 1968 it wasn't yet a federal crime to shoot a presidential candidate, so the Los Angeles Police Department (LAPD) took charge of the investigation into Kennedy's murder. With the FBI's assistance, they spent the next fourteen months investigating the murder.

From the beginning, the LAPD claimed the assassination was an open-and-shut case. Numerous witnesses had seen Sirhan Sirhan, the 24-year-old Palestinian immigrant who'd been apprehended at the crime scene, fire at Kennedy. Sirhan himself admitted he must have shot the Senator (since so many witnesses had seen him),

Sirhan Sirhan is taken into custody immediately after the shooting.

even though he couldn't remember anything about the evening from the time he'd had a cup of coffee with an attractive young woman until after he'd emptied his gun and lay pinned to the pantry steam table.

Sirhan also seemed to have a clear motive. When he was taken into custody, the police found in his pocket a newspaper clipping criticizing RFK for opposing the Vietnam War while favoring military aid to Israel. A background check revealed that as a young child in Palestine, Sirhan had seen the bloodied bodies of Arabs bombed by the Israelis, and his own brother was killed by an enemy truck as it veered to avoid sniper fire. Authorities reasoned that those early experiences had left Sirhan embittered against American politicians, like RFK, who supported Israel.

Even more incriminating was a notebook found in Sirhan's bedroom at his mother's house, in the Los Angeles suburb of Pasadena. It contained anti-American, pro-communist sentiments, and two pages of scrawled, repetitive references to killing RFK. The most damning of these read, "May 18 9:45 AM-68 My determination to eliminate RFK is becoming more the more [sic] of an unshakable obsession...RFK must die." (Sirhan acknowledged that the scrawls in the diary were his, but claimed he couldn't remember writing them.)

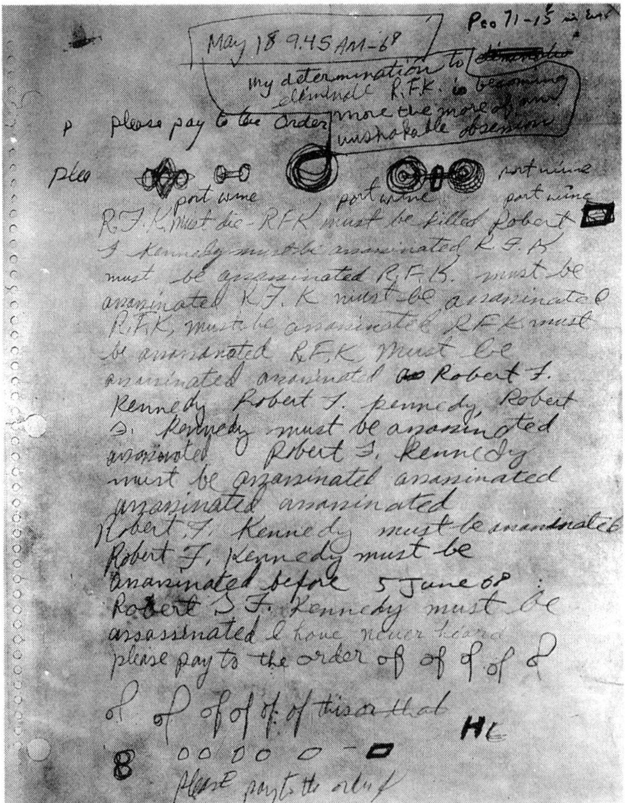
May 18 9.45 AM-68
my determination to eliminate R.F.K. is becoming more the more of an unshakable obsession
please pay to the order
plea
port wine port wine port wine port wine
R.F.K. must die - RFK must be killed Robert F. Kennedy must be assassinated R.F.K. must be assassinated R.F.K. must be assassinated R.F.K. must be assassinated R.F.K. must be assassinated RFK must be assassinated R.F.K. must be assassinated assassinated Robert F. Kennedy Robert F. Kennedy, Robert F. Kennedy must be assassinated assassinated Robert F. Kennedy must be assassinated assassinated assassinated assassinated Robert F. Kennedy must be assassinated Robert F. Kennedy must be assassinated before 5 June 68 Robert F. Kennedy must be assassinated I have never heard please pay to the order of of of of of of of of of of of this or that
please pay to the order of

UMD Archives

A page from Sirhan's notebook.

The LAPD was not only sure that Sirhan was the assassin—they were also sure he'd acted alone. In the early morning hours of June 5, several witnesses had gone on television or radio (or had told interviewing officers) about a suspicious woman in a polka-dot dress; she'd been seen with Sirhan before the shooting and fleeing the hotel with another man (or men) afterwards. But the police had decided that the woman wasn't connected to Sirhan. And since the LAPD ballistics report had supposedly accounted for all wounds with the bullets from Sirhan's gun, there was no reason to suspect a second gunman. There was, the LAPD claimed, no evidence to suggest conspiracy.

This view was never seriously challenged at Sirhan's trial. The prosecution believed they had a solid case against Sirhan, and talk about conspiracy was an unnecessary complication. Sirhan's lawyers reasoned that with so many witnesses to the shooting, the best they could do for their client was to plead diminished capacity and avoid the death penalty. That plea would be much harder to defend if it were shown that Sirhan had planned the crime with others.

So the trial focussed primarily on Sirhan's mental state—was this the spontaneous act of a psychologically disturbed young man, or did he plan the crime?

Defense attorney Emile Zola Berman argued that since Sirhan couldn't remember either shooting Kennedy or writing in his notebook, the killing must have been "without premeditation or malice, totally the product of a sick, obsessed mind and personality."

The prosecution rebutted with evidence of premeditation. Not only did Sirhan's notebook mention the plan to kill RFK, but he'd also been seen in two incriminating situations prior to the assassination. On June 2, when Kennedy made a pre-primary appearance at the Ambassador Hotel, Sirhan was seen there too—as if stalking his target. On the morning and afternoon of June 4, fifteen witnesses saw Sirhan at the San Gabriel Valley Gun Club, rapid-firing his .22 pistol—as if practicing for the kill.

Ultimately, the jury sided with the prosecution. They found Sirhan guilty of first-degree murder and sentenced him to death. The California Supreme Court upheld the conviction, but the US Supreme Court (in an unrelated case) declared the death penalty unconstitutional before Sirhan could be executed.

Sirhan was sent to San Quentin Prison in northern California. Now eligible for parole, he's been turned down several times (largely because, as one denial stated, his crime "disenfranchised millions of people").

The cover-up

From the beginning, a handful of journalists and citizens remained skeptical about the LAPD's conclusions. But when these critics tried to substantiate their suspicions with data from police files, they met massive resistance. The LAPD replied that the files were under lock-and-key, accessible only to those law-enforcement officials with a "need to know." The Los Angeles authorities even initiated legal proceedings against some critics who questioned the official findings.

Undaunted, two groups of concerned citizens prepared formal requests for disclosure. First, in 1975, CBS News and a group of petitioners filed the first disclosure request with the California Superior Court. The judge ruled against opening the files. Then, in 1984, political scientist Greg Stone, Paul Schrade, this author (and others) made a second attempt. On behalf of the Robert F. Kennedy Assassination Archives, housed at the University of Massachusetts, Dartmouth, we requested release of the files from both the Los Angeles District Attorney's office (LADA) and from the LAPD.

LADA began to process its files for disclosure the following year, but the LAPD continued to resist for three more years—

until letter campaigns and media coverage made it politically inexpedient to keep the information secret any longer. On April 19, 1988, the files were sent to the California State Archives in Sacramento, where researchers could evaluate the evidence for themselves.

The files made it clear that the LAPD had engaged in a massive cover-up, both during the original investigation and in the intervening twenty years. They'd not only attempted to misconstrue or overlook data that didn't support their lone-assassin view, but they'd actively destroyed evidence that might suggest a conspiracy. It had already been revealed in the first disclosure hearings that authorities had destroyed the hotel pantry ceiling tiles and the doorframe (both of which might have contained unaccounted-for bullets) in 1969. Now it was learned that:

- The results of the 1968 test firing of Sirhan's gun were missing.
- The test gun used for ballistics comparison and identification was destroyed.
- Over 90% of the audiotaped witness testimony was lost or destroyed. Of the 3470 interviews the LAPD conducted, only 301 were preserved. Key testimony—like 29 witness accounts that suggested conspiracy—was missing, while less important

interviews—like that of Sirhan's Bible teacher—remained.

- On August 21, 1968, less than two months after the assassination, 2400 photographs from the original investigation were burned, in the medical-waste incinerator at LA County General Hospital. The LAPD claimed that the photos were duplicates, but there weren't any known logs or inventories of photos that could verify that.

  Moreover, Scott Enyart, an amateur photographer who'd been taking pictures the night of the assassination and whose film had been confiscated by police, has never been given back all his photos. His pictures, the only ones that might have captured the actual shooting, weren't in the files.

But even with the limited data that remained, there was still ample evidence to substantiate what critics had been saying all along—that there was a conspiracy to kill RFK.

The evidence for such a conspiracy falls into three key areas. First, it now appears clear that it was impossible for Sirhan to have fired the bullets that killed Kennedy—which means there must have been a second gunman. Second, an abundance of testimony by eye-witnesses suggests that Sirhan had at least two accomplices. Third, Sirhan's political motive—his hatred of

RFK for supporting Israel—seems to be either a fabrication of the LAPD or a motive planted by conspirators to divert suspicion from a more sinister plot.

This book analyzes the evidence that's emerged in each of these three areas, and documents the LAPD's attempts to keep that truth from reaching the public eye.

Chapter 2

Evidence for a second gunman

When the numerous witnesses to the murder saw Sirhan raise his gun and fire—and then saw the Senator immediately react and fall to the ground—they naturally assumed that Sirhan had fired the shots that killed Kennedy. But when the witness testimony is compared with the autopsy and ballistics evidence, that conclusion becomes highly improbable.

The assassin's location

The autopsy revealed three gunshot wounds in Robert Kennedy's body—one behind the right ear, a second near the right armpit and a third 1½ inches below the armpit wound. A fourth bullet missed his body but pierced the right rear shoulder of his suit coat. All bullets entered from the right rear, at fairly steep upward angles and in a slightly right-to-left direction.

The bullets produced a dark, well-defined gunpowder burn on the Senator's head and clothing. When the LAPD test-fired a gun identical to Sirhan's (into pigs' ears to simulate flesh and into clothing similar to Kennedy's), they found that the burn could only be replicated if the gun

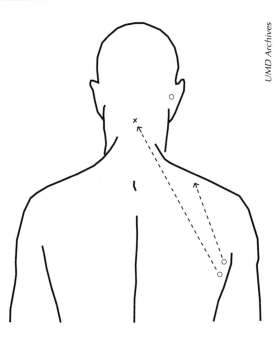

UMD Archives

This schematic drawing by Gregory Stone shows the paths of the bullets that hit RFK. Circles indicate where they entered, arrows indicate where they exited, and the X shows where a bullet lodged in his brain.

was fired at nearly point blank range. The LAPD concluded that "the bullet which entered behind Senator Kennedy's right ear was fired at a muzzle distance of approximately one inch." Coroner Thomas Naguchi concluded that the other wounds were inflicted at a distance of "contact" to "one inch" away.

The LAPD claimed that Sirhan was the gunman even though these findings conflicted with eyewitness testimony in four key ways. First, the prosecution's star witness, maître d' Karl Uecker, testified that he grabbed Sirhan's gun after the second shot, aiming it away from the Senator.

Another close eyewitness, assistant maître d' Edward Manasian, agreed. He told authorities, "I saw the first two shots fired....At that time Uecker hit [Sirhan's] arm and grabbed his...neck, [placed a] hold around his neck, and then I grabbed him from the left side." Although Sirhan emptied his gun of six more shots, none of these could've hit Kennedy.

Second, although witnesses disagree on whether Sirhan shot at RFK while the Senator was turned to his left shaking hands with busboy Juan Romero or whether the handshake had finished and Kennedy was walking forward, all agree that Sirhan approached Kennedy from the front and that the Senator never turned his back to Sirhan.

This is totally inconsistent with the autopsy evidence that the shots came from the rear. Even if Kennedy had been turned to the left, Sirhan wasn't in a position to shoot at his back—at most he could have wounded Kennedy's right temple or the side of his right ear.

Third, Sirhan couldn't have fired at Kennedy at point blank range. Uecker, who was standing in front and to the right of Kennedy, consistently asserted that Sirhan didn't get around him. All the witnesses agreed. All except one described Sirhan's gun as at least 1½ feet from Kennedy; most thought it was as far as 2 to 4 feet away.

At any of these distances, the powder burns wouldn't have appeared on the Senator's body. (Only *LA Times* photographer Boris Yaro said the gun was "inside a foot" of Kennedy's head. But Yaro was viewing the shooting through his camera lens—although not taking pictures—which may have distorted the distances.)

Fourth, even if Sirhan had somehow managed to get around to Kennedy's back, there are also problems with the angle and pattern of the wounds. To inflict the wounds at two levels (at the ear and armpit), Sirhan either had to move the gun and fire at Kennedy from two different levels, or Kennedy had to change position while Sirhan was firing.

Witnesses almost unanimously agreed that Sirhan fired with an outstretched arm, with the gun roughly parallel to the floor. The angle didn't change until Uecker grabbed Sirhan's arm. And although Kennedy's position did change—he fell backward to the floor—that would have made it even *more* difficult for Sirhan's gun to have inflicted Kennedy's wounds. Sirhan would have had to fire from his knees to achieve the upward angle reported in the autopsy.

Although some of this conflicting evidence emerged at Sirhan's trial, neither the prosecution or defense took much notice of it. The LAPD claimed that they had successfully reenacted the crime on film (two reconstructions were staged in 1968 and a third in 1977), and that the film proved their position was tenable— that Sirhan could get the gun one to three inches from the Senator and inflict four bullets at an upward-leftward angle, all before the gun was grabbed and deflected by Karl Uecker.

But when the Los Angeles DA's office began to release their files in 1985, a different story emerged. In the first 1968 reconstruction, Uecker was present. In the first takes in this series, Sirhan wasn't able to get access to inflict Kennedy's wounds. In two later takes, the Sirhan stand-in did get the gun behind the ear, but only when Kennedy moved his head awkwardly backward and slightly downward toward the gun (a movement not reported by any witnesses).

In the second 1968 reconstruction, Uecker wasn't present and his testimony was totally disregarded. With LA authorities playing all the roles, "Uecker" stood aside and let Sirhan rush past him to get to Kennedy. Kennedy turned slightly backward to shake hands, although witnesses placed him either facing forward or sideways—never backward.

Even with all this distortion, the best the actors could do was solve the distance problem. The proper angle for the wounds was never achieved, and nothing but a head wound (or wounds) was simulated.

In the 1977 series of reconstructions (using eyewitness Lisa Urso), none of the wounds could be simulated. So it's never been shown that it was possible for Sirhan to have fired the fatal shots at RFK. And if he didn't, there must have been a second gunman.

Ballistics

The LAPD relied on two kinds of ballistics evidence to support their lone-assassin view. First, they claimed that all testable bullet fragments recovered from victims' bodies matched bullets test fired from Sirhan's gun. Second, they claimed that bullet trajectories for the eight bullets Sirhan fired could account for all wounds to RFK and other pantry victims, and all other bullet damage at the crime scene.

The first claim can't be either substantiated or denied. It's true that all the bullets recovered from crime scene victims were .22 caliber—and Sirhan was firing a .22 handgun. But when a 1975 firearms panel tried to actually match the markings on the recovered bullets with those of bullets test fired from Sirhan's gun, the results were inconclusive.

That's because some of the bullets from Sirhan's gun were in poor physical condition "resulting from impact damage and/or fragmentation" and couldn't be tested; other bullets weren't marked sufficiently by the barrel of Sirhan's gun to compare them with test-fired bullets. So the panel couldn't prove that any of the bullets either did or didn't come from Sirhan's weapon.

The second LAPD claim is easier to dispute, because police criminologist DeWayne Wolfer's ballistics scenario is highly suspect. He accounted for all wounds and damage with the following eight bullet trajectories:

- Two bullets hit Kennedy and remained lodged in his body.

- A third bullet entered Kennedy's right back, exited his right front chest, passed through the ceiling tile and was lost in the ceiling interspace.

- A fourth bullet passed through the right shoulder of Kennedy's suit coat (never entering his body) and traveled upward, striking victim Paul Schrade in the center of his forehead.

- A fifth bullet struck Ira Goldstein's left hip.
- A sixth bullet entered Goldstein's left pant leg (never entering his body), hit the cement floor, then hit Erwin Stroll's left leg.
- A seventh bullet hit William Weisel in the stomach.
- An eighth bullet hit the ceiling tile, and then wounded Elizabeth Evans in the head.

Wolfer's report glosses over the fact that the proposed trajectories for the fourth, sixth and eighth bullets range from improbable to virtually impossible.

According to Wolfer, the fourth bullet passed through Kennedy's suit coat, travelling upward at approximately an 80-degree angle and striking Paul Schrade in the head. But the bullet passed from back to front, and all eyewitnesses place Kennedy in front of Schrade, with his back or side to his friend. Schrade claims he was four to five feet behind Kennedy, and that to fulfill Wolfer's scenario, he would've had "to be nine feet tall or have my head on Kennedy's shoulder."

Wolfer's sixth bullet is supposed to have gone cleanly through Ira Goldstein's pant leg, hit the cement floor, then deflected upward to lodge in Erwin Stroll's leg. But Goldstein testified to the grand jury that when the bullet passed through his pant leg, Stroll had already reacted to being hit and fallen to the floor.

Wolfer said the eighth bullet pierced a one-inch-thick ceiling tile, ricocheted off the inner ceiling, re-entered through the tile, and struck Elizabeth Evans in the head. But the medical report on Mrs. Evans described the bullet as entering "just below the hairline" and traveling "upward."

Equally suspicious is the fact that the bullet collided with the hard surface above the ceiling tile without fragmenting or mushrooming and retained three-fourths of its original weight (making it akin to the "magic bullet" described by the Warren Commission in the JFK assassination).

Even if these trajectories were valid (which they're clearly not), Wolfer's whole theory goes out the window if other bullets were found lodged in the ceiling or the doorframe of the pantry. If even one more bullet was discovered, that means there had to be a second gun.

After the assassination, the LAPD removed any suspicious ceiling tiles and sections of the door frame to probe for bullets. They officially admitted that there were three holes in the ceiling tile, which they claimed were made by Wolfer's third and eighth bullets (the eighth bullet is supposed to have made two holes—one when entering the tile and the other deflecting back into the room).

But other evidence suggests there were more holes than that. Eyewitness Lisa Urso recalled that just after the shooting she looked up at the ceiling and was surprised to see what appeared to be "bullet holes" (she doesn't remember how many).

When she returned to the pantry three hours later (authorities hadn't noticed her and so she hadn't been put in a holding room to await interviewing, as had the other eyewitnesses), she noticed that five or six tiles had been removed from the ceiling and placed on the floor. Police officers were poking around—looking for bullets, she thought. She looked down at two of the tiles nearest her and saw three holes in one tile and one in another.

Her report is corroborated by LAPD crime scene photos showing numerous ceiling tiles removed, and even by LAPD Deputy Chief Robert Houghton's 1970 book *Special Unit Senator* (which upheld the official view). There Houghton quotes Wolfer as saying, "It's unbelievable how many holes there are in the kitchen ceiling." And yet a police property report, curiously dated 22 days after the property was booked into evidence, describes only two ceiling tiles removed.

Then there's the pantry doorframe. The official story is that there were no bullet holes there, but numerous investigators and witnesses disagree. Here's a sampling of their testimony (much of which has been collected by independent researchers):

LAPD crime scene photos show Wolfer pointing to a spot on the upper doorframe. In a 1971 deposition, he implied that the photo showed a bullet hole. He stated: "We wouldn't photograph just any hole. I mean, there were too many holes to photograph."

LA coroner Dr. Thomas Noguchi confirmed that Wolfer found bullets at the scene. In a 1975 affadavit to Vincent Bugliosi (the Charles Manson prosecutor who independently re-investigated the RFK case), Noguchi said: "I asked Mr. Wolfer where he had found bullet holes at the scene....He pointed, as I recall, to one hole in a ceiling panel above, and an indentation in the cement ceiling. He also pointed to several holes in the door frames of the swinging doors leading into the pantry."

LAPD officers Robert Rozzi and Charles Wright were shown in an AP photo kneeling near a hole in the doorframe. In a 1975 affadavit, Rozzi told Bugliosi that he saw "a hole in the door jamb, and the base of what appeared to be a small caliber bullet was lodged in the hole." In a telephone conversation with Bugliosi, Charles Wright confirmed that a bullet "was definitely removed from the hole, but I don't know who did it." (Wright later refused to confirm the telephone conversation or to provide a statement.)

Witness Martin Patruski also gave an affadavit to Bugliosi. Patruski stated that "one of the officers pointed to two circled holes on the center divider of the swinging doors and told us that they had dug two bullets out of the center divide....I am absolutely sure that the police told us that two bullets were dug out of these holes."

Retired 15-year FBI veteran William Bailey, who worked at the RFK crime scene, has consistently maintained that "there were at least two bullet holes in the center post....Short of actually taking the wood off myself and examining it, I would say that I'm reasonably certain they were bullet holes. I've seen bullet holes in wood before. I looked into these holes....They were definitely not nail holes. There appeared to be objects inside." Photos released by the FBI in 1976 under a Freedom of Information Act request corroborate Bailey's view: four separate holes were labelled as "bullet holes."

Two hotel carpenters, Dale Poore and Wesley Harrington, helped authorities remove the doorframe. In interviews conducted by the DA's office in 1975, both men described what they thought were bullet holes. Poore stated: "It looked like the bullet had went in at sort of an angle as it was travelling this way. So it made a bit of an oblong hole and the fiber of the board had closed in some after it went in. And that's the only reason I thought it had been a bullet went in there, because you put any kind of a metal instrument, punch nail sets, anything in the hole, it won't have a fiber around the edge."

In response to the question "Would you be comfortable with using language that said [the holes in the doorframe] actually were bullet holes?," Harrington replied, "Yes, I would. During my teenage years...we had use of air rifles and .22 rifles and we had fired into old buildings and trees, and this looked like a hole similar to a small caliber bullet."

Karl Uecker, in a 1990 oral history interview with California State Archivist John Burns, revealed for the first time that he'd seen what appeared to be two bullet holes in the center divider of the pantry doorway. He passed through the door dozens of times each night and was sure he would've seen the holes if they'd existed previously.

When asked why he thought they were bullet holes, Uecker responded: "Because these holes never were there before and I knew where the shots were going to." Uecker recalls pointing the holes out to a man whom he thought to be a plainclothes policeman. The man responded that everything would be checked out.

In the spring of 1990, investigative journalist Dan Moldea did what LA officials had failed to do—he attempted to talk to all of the law-enforcement personnel involved at the crime scene. He actually succeeded in interviewing over 100 LAPD officers and sheriff's deputies. His May 13, 1990 article in the *Washington Post* provided new evidence that extra bullets existed:

- LAPD photographer Charles Collier was asked if he was sure that the holes he photographed were bullet holes. He answered, "A bullet hole looks like a bullet hole if you've photographed enough of them." (Only 51 of 98 Collier photos allegedly took at the crime scene have been accounted for.)

- Patrolman Al Lamoreaux told Moldea, "I do recall seeing one or two holes in the door around wherever he had just shot him...it was just obvious. Just being a dumb cop you look and see where the bullets went."

- Sergeant James MacArthur, the senior police detective at the crime scene, told Moldea he had seen "quite a few" bullet holes, including one high on the wall to the left of the swinging doors.

- Officer Kenneth E. Vogel stated that he was positive he saw two .22 bullet fragments on the pantry floor, and he brought his discovery to the attention of another LAPD official. No such fragments were ever reported or booked into evidence, according to released LAPD files.

- Sergeant Raymond Rolon told Moldea, "One of the investigators pointed to a hole in the doorframe and said, 'We just pulled a bullet out of here.'"

- Deputy Sheriff Thomas Beringer recalled a man in a tuxedo "trying to take a bullet out of the [doorframe] with a knife, a silver knife, for a souvenir."

The LAPD's response to the question of extra bullets was to conduct a systematic cover-up. As mentioned above, they destroyed the ceiling tiles and doorframe wood in 1969, as well as records of tests done on the door frames or ceiling tiles. Then, when photos of this crucial area were released, they were identified only by number but lacked captions or labelling. Since there's no corresponding log to indicate what the numbers refer to, they aren't of much use as evidence.

When the destruction of the evidence was revealed in 1975, the LAPD claimed that they'd destroyed the tiles and frame wood because they were "too large to fit into a card file" (needless to say, so is a lot of evidence). Daryl Gates, who at that point was assistant chief of police, claimed that the destruction didn't matter because the tiles and frame wood contained no bullets and therefore weren't evidence.

The DA's office attempted to dispel mounting public suspicion by conducting what critics would dub "the great pantry raid." Investigators descended upon the crime scene to conduct a meticulous search for bullets and bullet holes. Ignoring the fact that the most relevant holes (in the door jamb and ceiling tiles) had been removed and destroyed seven years earlier, they concluded that the one supposedly surviving hole (which in 1968 had allegedly been labelled as a bullet hole) was in fact a nail hole. The day after the raid, an official spokesman dramatically announced that "no other bullets were found last night."

Eyewitness reports

Los Angeles officials like to argue that if there'd been a second gun in the pantry, someone in the crowd of more than 70 witnesses would've seen it. There are several problems with that reasoning.

First, it downplays the confusion at the crime scene. This wasn't an event witnessed by over 70 people who were watching Kennedy at center stage and suddenly saw him attacked. Many people didn't see the shooting at all, while others thought the noise came from bursting balloons or firecrackers. Some saw Kennedy reel or fall but had no view of the gun or assailant; some saw Sirhan but not his gun, and some saw the gun and not Sirhan.

Moreover, the majority of witnesses in Kennedy's area didn't report seeing the uniformed security guard on Kennedy's right, Thane Cesar, draw his gun (as he claims he did). So the possibility of a second gun can't be dismissed by the notion that everyone would have seen it.

Second, the LAPD's argument overlooks the fact that witnesses might have seen another gun but not reported it. One reason for their silence could be that many witnesses mistakenly thought Kennedy was guarded by US Secret Service. For them, other guns would seem natural and appropriate.

Another reason is that the LAPD discouraged testimony about a second gunman from the first round of police interviews, within hours of the shooting. In these first interviews, witnesses were never questioned about other guns; instead, the LAPD asked highly structured questions that focused almost solely on Sirhan. This animosity to testimony about a second gun continued through the investigation and trial and on to the subsequent "reinvestigations."

Later, most witnesses believed that the one-gun conclusion had been solidly established, and that other information was irrelevant. I've since been told by two credible witnesses that they didn't volunteer observations that we now know are important. These witnesses have requested to remain anonymous, but their detailed statements exist on audio tape or, in one case, in a sworn affidavit. They're also ready to testify before the next official reinvestigation.

One witness, for example, told me that she'd seen a Caucasian man in a suit (not a uniform) shoot a handgun "once or twice" before running out of the pantry. She described him as about 6'2" tall, with dark, wavy hair. Another witness saw a man in a suit standing close to Kennedy; he was firing a gun at an upward angle.

It's also possible that others saw a gun but were afraid to talk. The widely publicized mysterious deaths of scores of witnesses to President Kennedy's assassination might have had a chilling effect on witnesses in both this and the Martin Luther King assassination.

Third, and most important, the LAPD seems to have forgotten the fact that three witnesses did report a second gun early on, but were ignored. One witness told me he'd seen a man in a suit fire shots; the witness gave chase as the man and a woman fled the pantry. The authorities tried to explain away the gun by saying it was carried by a security guard or a secret service agent (even though presidential candidates weren't given secret service protection in 1968).

When I interviewed Lisa Urso, a key eyewitness, she clearly recalled someone she assumed to be a "security guard" (though he wasn't in uniform) drawing a gun. She sighted the gun immediately after the shooting, just as Sirhan's gun was wrestled from him. She mentioned this "guard" to the authorities on a couple of occasions, but they didn't seem interested.

Don Schulman, a runner for KNXT-TV in Los Angeles, also reported seeing a gun other than Sirhan's. He'd been standing behind Kennedy as he walked through the pantry and had seen a security guard fire three times. Immediately after the shooting, Schulman reported his story on the radio and insisted that Kennedy was shot three times. Even though the early media reports and crime-scene witnesses generally asserted that the Senator was hit only twice, Schulman stuck to his story. The autopsy proved him right.

(In later law-enforcement interviews, when Schulman was under pressure to be "absolutely positive" about what he saw,

Schulman stated that he didn't see the guard shoot Kennedy, as his first statement seemed to imply. He did assert that he saw the guard fire three times and Kennedy hit three times, but admitted he couldn't necessarily connect the two events.)

The Cesar controversy

If there was a second gunman, who was it? One likely candidate is Thane Cesar, the uniformed security guard walking close behind Kennedy.

Some facts about Cesar certainly look suspicious. First, although Cesar claims to have worked for Ace Guard service (a service often used by the Ambassador Hotel) for more than six months before the assassination, Ace records shown to independent journalists indicated that he was only hired in May 1968.

Second, William Gardner, chief of security for the Ambassador, had assigned Cesar to the pantry area at either 9:30 or 10:50 pm (there are conflicting accounts), to prevent people from entering the overcrowded Embassy Room via the kitchen. Yet even though several others noticed Sirhan in the pantry area before the shooting, Cesar claimed that he didn't see anyone loitering or looking suspicious, and that he'd never seen Sirhan before the shooting.

Third, it's not clear why Cesar was walking close beside Kennedy, who hadn't wanted any armed or uniformed guards nearby. Caesar claimed that his close proximity to Kennedy was serendipitous: "As he walked through, for some reason I just....We started walking with him and I happened to wind up on his right side....Just as he passed me, I followed him."

Fourth, Caesar offered conflicting accounts about when and how he drew his gun, and about what happened to him during the shooting. Within hours of the event, he told the LAPD "I went for [my gun] but it was too late. He had done [sic] fired five shots and when he did, I ducked because I was as close as Kennedy was. I fell against [the ice machine] and then the Senator fell right down in front of me." Almost a week later, Cesar told the FBI a different version—that he'd been knocked over before drawing his gun and drew it as he scrambled to his feet.

In the first interview, Cesar also indicated that he'd fallen on his own; three weeks later he told the LAPD that maître d' Karl Uecker had knocked him against the ice box. Uecker's most detailed accounts never mention colliding with anyone but Sirhan.

Fifth, although Cesar maintains that he carried only the required .38 revolver that night (and there's no evidence to the contrary), the matter is complicated by the fact that Cesar did own a .22 handgun (the same kind Sirhan used), and there's conflicting information about when he got rid of it. In 1971, Cesar told authorities that he'd sold the .22 prior to the assassination. But while researching the assassination for his film, *The Second Gun,* Ted Charach contacted Jim Yoder, who bought the gun from Cesar. Yoder produced a receipt, signed by Cesar, that was dated September 1968.

Sixth, within minutes after the shooting, Cesar was interviewed by John Marshall of KFWB radio in Los Angeles. When asked about Kennedy's wounds, Cesar replied that Kennedy had been hit in the head, chest and shoulder and that there'd been four shots. That makes Cesar the only person besides Schulman to correctly state that Kennedy was hit three times. But Cesar seemed to know even more than Schulman—he knew (or did he guess?) the location of the wounds.

How could he have known? If, as he claimed, he ducked or was knocked down early in the shooting, he would have fallen at about the same time as Kennedy. The Senator landed on his back, concealing the location of his wounds. Nobody who looked down on Kennedy as he lay there, including the first doctor to reach his side, reported the correct number of wounds.

Seventh, Cesar's right-wing political views, antipathy toward the Kennedy family and alleged mob contacts have caused some to speculate that he had motive to kill Kennedy. For example, Cesar supported the presidential candidacy of George Wallace in 1968 and talked of the possibility of a race war in the US (resulting from integration policies).

In a 1987 interview with researcher Dan Moldea, Cesar expressed his feelings about the Kennedys: "I had no use for the Kennedy family...I've read a lot of books on [them] and I think they're the biggest bunch of crooks that ever walked the earth." And researcher Alex Botus claims that Cesar has been connected to alleged California mobster John Alessio.

But there are also arguments against Cesar's involvement. First, he cooperated fully with authorities and appeared to be candid in telling his own story. Even though that story is convoluted, he doesn't try to rework it in his own best interests. He doesn't, for example, try to put Sirhan at point-blank range with the gun behind Kennedy.

Second, Moldea couldn't find any evidence to substantiate claims of Cesar's Mafia contacts or history of contract chores for the mob. Moldea also pointed out that Cesar hasn't appeared to prosper in any significant way since the shooting.

Third, even though Cesar's political views have made him a target of some conspiracy theorists, he hasn't tried to downplay or change those views in any way.

Finally, since four witness saw a man in a suit either holding or firing a gun (as mentioned in the preceding section), it's clear that Cesar isn't the only candidate for a second gunman.

So the conflicting, inadequate data surrounding Cesar doesn't solidly support the conclusion that he was the second gunman. But neither does it support the official conclusion that all questions about him have been satisfactorily answered. His role needs to be investigated further.

Chapter 3

Possible accomplices

The woman in the polka-dot dress

More helpful information about the crime might come from the young woman whom many witnesses reported seeing with Sirhan—either in the two weeks preceding the assassination or at the Ambassador Hotel on June 4. Because so many witnesses identified her by the dress she was wearing at the hotel, she's become known as the "woman in the polka-dot dress" (or, in the parlance of the 60s, "the polka-dot-dress girl").

Sirhan was spotted with this light-haired woman three times prior to the assassination. On May 20, Albert LeBeau was taking tickets for a 400-guest Kennedy fund-raising luncheon at a Pomona restaurant. Hearing a commotion on the stairway behind him, he turned to see a young woman and man (later identified as Sirhan) climbing over a brick facade and railing to get into the dining room. LeBeau described the woman as "Caucasian, 25 to 30 years old, with medium blond, shoulder-length hair." She seemed "about 5'6"—somewhat taller than the man"—and had a "nice shape, built proportionately."

When LeBeau asked for their tickets, the couple claimed to be "with the Senator's party." LeBeau refused to admit them, and then lost sight of them in the crowd. But the couple somehow managed to get into the luncheon anyway; LeBeau later saw them standing against the back wall of the dining room, listening to Kennedy's speech.

On May 30, Laverne Botting was working at Kennedy campaign headquarters in Azusa, an LA suburb, when two men and a woman entered the office. A man whom she would later identify as "Sirhan or a person who very closely resemble[d] Sirhan" approached her desk and asked whether Senator Kennedy would be visiting the area; she responded that he wouldn't. Botting described the woman as a "22-year-old Caucasian, 5'7" tall, slim," with an "excellent figure and dishwater blond" hair. She didn't describe the other man.

Ethel Creehan overhead the brief exchange between Botting and the man (she also later felt "fairly certain" it was Sirhan). Creehan described the woman as thin, perhaps 19, but with "makeup that made her appear 23 to 25." She had "brown or blond hair and a prominent nose."

On June 4, between 5:00 and 5:30 pm, Sirhan and a young woman were again seen at Kennedy campaign headquarters—this time at the Los Angeles office on

Wilshire Boulevard. Khaiber Khan, an Iranian immigrant and Kennedy volunteer, saw a man he'd later recognize as Sirhan standing near the water cooler, facing a young woman. Khan didn't see them talk, but had the impression they were together.

The woman caught Khan's attention because he'd seen her twice before—he'd noticed her earlier that same afternoon and also the day before, when she'd been sitting in a Volkswagen with a well-dressed man (not Sirhan) outside campaign headquarters. As he passed the car, Khan heard the man say, "I just spoke with Lilli Lawrence. But Lilli said it was impossible." Khan later told the FBI that he knew a Lilli Lawrence, an Iranian woman married to an American. The man in the VW somewhat resembled an acquaintance of hers whom Khan had met in New York.

Khan described the woman as in her "early twenties, 120 to 125 pounds, with light brown or dark blond shoulder-length hair, large dark eyes, a round face, and a good figure and nice legs." On June 4, she was wearing a "short-sleeved dress with black or blue polka dots."

On the day of the assassination, fifteen witnesses claimed to have seen Sirhan rapidly firing his .22 pistol for hours at the San Gabriel Valley Gun Club in Duarte, about fifteen miles from Los Angeles. Three of the witnesses also saw a couple—a young blond woman and another man (not Sirhan) at the club.

Gun club employees Harry Hicks and Russell Doyle Weaver saw a man and woman arrive shortly after 11 am. Hicks remembered the woman as "quite shapely" and joked about her good looks with Weaver. Weaver described the woman as "18 to 19 years old, 5'2" to 5'3" tall, 100 pounds, with blond hair."

Everett Buckner, the range master, also reported that a couple entered the gun club. He thought it was between 10:00 and 10:30 am, shortly after Sirhan had checked in. The couple had a rifle and what Buckner believed to be a .22 pistol. The woman was "young, blond and attractive."

While the man fired the rifle on the rifle range, the woman fired a .22 pistol on another range near Sirhan. She was having difficulty firing the pistol, and Sirhan offered to help. Buckner claimed that she blurted out loud enough for him to hear, "God damn you, you son of a bitch, get out of here or they'll recognize us." Sirhan didn't leave, but continued to instruct her.

On the night of the assassination, a dozen witnesses at the Ambassador Hotel reported encountering a woman in a polka-dot dress. She was either alone, with a man they later identified as Sirhan or with a second, unidentified man.

Lonny L. Worthy was getting a soft drink for his wife just after 10 pm, when he bumped into Sirhan at the bar. A few minutes later Worthy noticed him standing next to a woman and thought they were together. There's no description of the woman in the FBI's interview summary.

Kennedy volunteer Susan Locke remembered a woman who seemed "somewhat out of place" in the Embassy Room just prior to Kennedy's speech; she was standing "expressionless" while the rest of the crowd celebrated. Locke described her as "Caucasian, in her early twenties and well-proportioned"; she had "long brown hair pulled back and was wearing a polka-dot dress." Since the woman didn't have a yellow badge (which was necessary for admission to the ballroom), Locke notified a nearby worker, who in turn notified a guard. It's not known if the guard responded or not.

Booker Griffin also saw the woman in the Embassy Room. It was about 10:30 pm, and she was standing next to a man whom Griffin later identified as Sirhan. The two weren't talking but Griffin had the impression they were together; they both seemed "totally out of the mood of the rest of the people." Griffin described the woman as of "Nordic descent" and taller than Sirhan. She wore a "predominantly white dress that may have had another color on it."

About 11:35 pm Griffin saw the same couple again, standing in the kitchen corridor. This time a third man was with them. He had a lighter complexion than Sirhan and was 6' to 6'2" tall. When the shooting occurred about 40 minutes later, Griffin saw the woman and taller man again, running out of the pantry. He blurted out, "They're getting away."

George Green was also in the kitchen corridor before the shooting, and had seen Sirhan standing near a tan, thin man and blond female Caucasian. The woman appeared to be in her "early twenties [and] wore a white dress with black polka dots"; she had long blond hair and a "good figure."

When Green entered the pantry after the shooting began, he noticed a man and woman running out of the pantry. They were conspicuous because everyone else seemed to be trying to get in. Green didn't say that this was the same woman he'd seen earlier (probably because he couldn't see the woman's face) but he described her in the same way—as in her early twenties, with long blond hair and a polka-dot dress.

Inside the pantry, prior to the shooting, others had noticed a woman with Sirhan. Vincent Di Pierro reported seeing Sirhan standing next to an attractive woman in a "polka-dot dress." Darnell Johnson, a Kennedy campaign worker who walked ahead of the Senator into the pantry, noticed a group of "five people" (four men and a woman) standing close to one another. He described two of the men and the woman.

One man was "6'1", blond, Caucasian...[and] wearing a light blue sport coat." The other was later identified as Sirhan. The woman was a "white female wearing a white dress with quarter-sized black polka dots." She was "23 to 25 years old, had long, light-brown hair, was 5'8" tall, weighed about 145 pounds and was well built."

When the shooting occurred, Johnson saw the woman and three men leave the pantry. While Sirhan was being held, before the police arrived, Johnson saw the polka-dot-dress woman and the man in the blue coat look into the pantry. He also claimed to see the woman again in the Embassy Room as Sirhan was taken out.

Four other witnesses saw the woman fleeing the pantry. Jack Merritt, one of the Senator's eight uniformed security guards, noticed "two men and a woman leaving the kitchen through the back exit." He didn't get a good look at the woman's face, but she was approximately "5'5" tall, had light-colored hair and wore a polka-dot dress." The two men wore suits and "seemed to be smiling."

Richard Houston also saw a woman wearing a "black-and-white polka-dot dress" with "ruffles around the neck and front." As she ran out of the pantry, he heard her say, "we killed him."

Evan Freed, a freelance photographer, had been knocked over when the crowd in the pantry scrambled to get out of the line of fire. He picked himself up in time to see two men and a woman running to a pantry exit. One man wore a light blue sport coat; Freed thought he was being chased by the other man. Freed didn't describe the woman except to say that she was "possibly wearing a polka-dot dress."

Marcus McBroom had run from the pantry into the Embassy Room after the shooting, hoping to find a doctor. On his way out of the pantry he noticed a woman in a "polka-dot dress," who seemed to be "calmer than everyone else" and "appeared to be trying to leave the room as soon as possible." She was "Caucasian, dark-haired, about 25 years old, 5'4" tall and 126 pounds."

Minutes after the shooting, three more witnesses sighted the woman in the polka-dot dress and another man fleeing the hotel. Sandra Serrano, a 20-year-old Kennedy worker, had left the crowded Embassy Room sometime before RFK's speech. She was trying to escape the heat and took refuge on an outside stairway. At about 11:30 pm, two men and a woman climbed up the stairs; Serrano moved aside so they could get past.

Serrano continued to sit there for more than half an hour; no one else came by. Then she heard what she thought were six car "backfires," four or five of which seemed close together. Moments later a man and a woman—two of the trio she had seen coming up the stairs earlier—came running down the stairs toward her. The woman said, "We shot him! We shot him!" Serrano asked: "Who did you shoot?" The woman replied, "Senator Kennedy."

Serrano later described the woman as "Caucasian, 23 to 27 years old, 5'6" tall, with dark brown hair." She was wearing a "white dress with black, quarter-inch polka dots." Serrano later identified Sirhan as the man who'd been with the couple when they first went up the stairs into the hotel.

Serrano's report is corroborated by an older couple, who are known only as "the Bernsteins." The couple had been near the exit stairs of the hotel when a young woman in a polka-dot dress and man ran past blurting, "We shot him!" We shot him!" When the couple asked, "Who did you shoot?" the young woman replied "Senator Kennedy." The Bernsteins, nearly hysterical, started to leave the hotel when they encountered LAPD Sergeant Paul Schraga in the parking lot and told him their story. (Schraga had heard of the shooting on his police radio and raced to the parking lot to set up a "command post.")

These descriptions of Sirhan's female companion do conflict at times. For example, witnesses described her hair color as anywhere from blond to dark brown. And Darnell Johnson's account of seeing the woman in the Embassy Room after Sirhan had been taken into custody conflicts with those who saw her flee the hotel minutes after the shooting. Yet there are also strong similarities in their testimonies. She's consistently described as being in her early to mid-twenties, having long hair and a good figure, and wearing a polka-dot dress.

The lady vanishes

What's most disturbing about the accounts of Sirhan's female companion is the way in which they were overlooked or discredited by the LAPD. The coverup began immediately after the assassination. After Sergeant Schraga encountered the Bernsteins in the parking lot, he went to his car and put out an All Points Bulletin (APB) on the two suspects who'd fled the hotel.

But the APB was mysteriously cancelled. At 1:41 am, an officer called the LAPD dispatcher to see if there was still a suspect at large. The dispatcher told the officer to "Disregard that [APB]. We got Rafer Johnson and Jesse Unruh who were right next to [Kennedy], and they only have one man and don't want them to get anything started on a big conspiracy." Even later, when it was clear that Sandra Serrano had also seen the couple flee the hotel, no one followed up on the Bernsteins. They were never interviewed, and Schraga's report with their names and address later disappeared from the files.

When the LAPD interviewed witnesses who'd seen Sirhan and a female companion either prior to or on the night of the assassination, the police either failed to include the information in their reports or tried to discredit the testimony. For example, in most of the LAPD interviews a female companion simply isn't mentioned; we only know about her because she appears in FBI interview summaries of the same witnesses.

In the few instances in which she's mentioned in the LAPD interviews, that information is usually absent from the LAPD *Summary Report* (which is supposed to sum up all interviews). If she does get mentioned in the *Summary Report,* the witness who sighted her is usually discredited.

Take, for example, the LAPD's response to Booker Griffin's testimony of three different sightings of Sirhan and a female companion. Rather than trying to pursue Griffin's lead, or attempting to corroborate his account with other witnesses, the LAPD discouraged Griffin's testimony with the "100-percent-certain" test (which was only used on people whose accounts implied a conspiracy or contradicted the official findings).

Griffin was asked: "If your life depended on it, that we're gonna send this man to the electric chair in another set of circumstances, could you say without any reservations, definitely, positively that this was the same man [Sirhan, on all three occasions]...no mistake about it?"

Griffin replied: "No, I wouldn't."

"How about the girl?"

"No."

"So if we're dealing with the facts now, you couldn't definitely say that she [the woman fleeing the pantry] was the same woman you saw earlier?"

"No."

The policeman then put words in Booker's mouth: "So the description you gave me earlier then was not really a description of what you saw then [the woman fleeing the pantry], but rather a projection from the girl that you had seen earlier." According to the *Summary Report*, Griffin agreed.

But the audio tape of this interview reveals an important difference between the *Summary* and Griffin's actual words. Although Griffin said he couldn't be absolutely sure it was the same woman in all three instances, he never inferred that there were possibly three different women, or that he may have mentally projected a composite.

When I interviewed Griffin in 1987, and showed him the recently released *Summary Report*, he reacted with disbelief, then anger: "I am a trained newsperson and I had been taught to watch details....I'm not blind. I'm not a dishonest person. I know what I saw." Later, he emphasized: "I have not recanted a statement. I will not recant a statement." Concerning his treatment by the LAPD, Griffin recalled: "They really tried very hard to break me down and lead me, as opposed to listen to me."

As heavy-handed as the LAPD's treatment of Griffin appears, it pales in comparison to their treatment of witness Sandra Serrano—the campaign worker who said she'd seen a couple fleeing the hotel.

The police initially showed a lot of interest in Serrano's story, perhaps because her story had been broadcast on national television shortly after the shooting. She was first interviewed by the LAPD on 2:35 am on the morning of the shooting, re-interviewed at 4:00 am and again on June 7. She was interviewed two more times during the next three days, and taken to police headquarters to further identify the couple who'd fled the hotel. She also participated in a video-taped reconstruction of her story and watched a staged fashion show of eight polka-dot dresses.

On June 20, she had her sixth interview, this time with LAPD Lt. Enrique Hernandez.

At this interview she allegedly failed a lie-detector test and finally agreed to what Hernandez had been insisting—that her story was false. But when the tape of this interview was released twenty years later, the real story emerged.

During the first part of the interview, Sandra's aunt was present, and Hernandez was cordial and sympathetic. He credited Sandra with being an "intelligent young woman" and invited her to tell her story "as best she can remember." He explained the workings of the polygraph she was to take, and the fact that it was thoroughly reliable.

Later in the interview, after Serrano's aunt had left, Hernandez took a different approach. He first tried to flatter Sandra, saying that she was one of the few witnesses whose motives for speaking out were pure. He claimed that nineteen women had come forward with stories, but most were gold diggers or publicity hounds. Only two, including Sandra, "really loved Kennedy as a person."

The fact that her motive was pure, he seemed to imply, made it all the more imperative that she recognize her story was mistaken. "You owe it to Senator Kennedy, the late Senator Kennedy, to come forward [and admit your story is wrong]. Be a woman about this. You don't know if he's a witness right now in this room. Don't shame his death by keeping this up."

He then played on her feelings for the Kennedys, who've had "nothing but tragedy. They must be satisfied. It [unintelligible] them to know the truth...And I'm sure—you mark my words—that one of these days, if you're woman enough, you will get a letter from Ethel Kennedy—personal—thanking you for at least letting her rest on these aspects of this investigation."

Serrano, occasionally feisty, made several attempts to hold her ground: "I'm not gonna say nobody told me ['we shot him'] just to satisfy anybody else."

"This didn't happen," Hernandez replied.

"It happened," she replied.

"No, it didn't happen....Nobody told you, 'we shot him,'" said Hernandez.

"Yes," she said, her voice almost inaudible.

"No," insists Hernandez.

"I'm sorry, but that's true. That is true," stated Serrano.

Hernandez finally won. Serrano admitted, under guided questioning, that her account was wrong. She claimed that she'd felt compelled to give more information that she actually had, and then couldn't admit the lie because she was afraid of appearing foolish.

Serrano's ordeal didn't end in 1968. When the files were released 20 years later, the press reported that Serrano had told the LAPD, "the whole thing was a lie." But three days after the documents were released, Sandra Serrano Sewell surfaced to tell radio interviewer Jack Thomas her side of the story. "There was a lot of badgering that was going on. I was just 20 years old and I became unglued....I said what they wanted me to say."

The barmaid and the spy-master

In their attempt to make the woman in the polka-dot dress disappear, the LAPD also failed to adequately follow up two other provocative leads. On June 6, Deborah Jaimison (a pseudonym to protect her identity) called the LAPD to say that Sirhan had been next to her shooting at the gun club on June 4. When the police finally interviewed her on June 19, it turned out that she closely matched the description of the shapely, long-haired blond woman who'd been at the firing range with Sirhan.

And yet there were some interesting discrepancies between Deborah Jaimison's story and those of other witnesses at the gun club. While she claimed that she and her husband had arrived at about 4 pm, other witnesses sighted someone like Deborah there in the morning. And two witnesses who claimed to have been at the range from 3:45 to 4:45 pm said that they didn't see Sirhan or any women on the range at that time.

That means that either the witnesses were incorrect about a couple arriving in the morning, that there's an unaccounted-for mystery couple who looked generally like the Jaimisons (but wasn't mentioned by the vast majority of the other 37 people present at the gun club that day) or that Jaimison's story is inaccurate.

Had the LAPD probed Deborah's story further, they would've discovered some potential connections between her and Sirhan. Deborah worked as a "barmaid-waitress" at the Briar Patch Bar, a topless bar three-quarters of a mile from the Santa Anita Racetrack, where Sirhan groomed horses from October 1965 to the spring of 1966. Sirhan's background file indicated he frequented topless bars, like the Cat Patch, which is only eight miles from the Briar Patch.

So it's possible Sirhan and Deborah Jaimison might have had contact before that day on the firing range, and that there was some basis for Buckner's claim that they seemed to know one another. But since the LAPD chose not to pursue the story, we can't reach a sound conclusion.

A second lead might have taken the LAPD beyond the polka-dot-dress story, perhaps into the realm of international espionage.

When the FBI followed up on Khaiber Khan's story (he was the Kennedy volunteer who'd seen a blond woman at the Wilshire Boulevard headquarters three times prior to the assassination), they found an interesting discrepancy.

Two other workers at the headquarters, Ellenor Severson and Larry Strick, had seen Sirhan there (without a blond companion) at about 2:00 pm on June 2; they also asserted that Khan was present at that time. Strick claimed he'd asked Sirhan if he needed help, and Sirhan had replied, "I'm with him," pointing to Khan. Severson corroborated Strick's story. But Khan claimed that he wasn't at headquarters at that time, that he couldn't remember any such incident and that he'd never seen Sirhan before the assassination.

When the FBI and the LAPD began to pursue this angle of the case, they found that Khan had an interesting history. According to their files, he'd once been influential in the Iranian government and had later fled to the US to escape the Shah. Lately he'd been working at the local Kennedy headquarters, recruiting young volunteers for the campaign.

While this information on Khan's background was true, it was incomplete. In a 1965 article in *The Nation,* Fred J. Cook revealed important facets of Khan's life that never appeared in the official files. In 1944, at age 20, Khan joined British intelligence and ran an Iranian spy ring. After World War II, he served as a liaison between the occupying allied forces in Iran and several Iranian tribes, and was awarded an aristocratic title for his efforts.

Cook credited Khan with helping the CIA overthrow Iranian Premier Mohammed Mossadegh in 1953. The coup rid the US of the left-leaning premier who'd nationalized a British oil company and put a puppet ruler, Shah Reza Pahlavi, in power.

According to Cook, Khan achieved great power in Iran, until a falling out with the Shah sent him into exile in London. From there he lived an opulent lifestyle, directing his spies to gather damaging evidence about the Shah's finances. In 1963, he entered the US; shortly afterwards, he was able to document the Shah's theft of US foreign aid and bring this to the attention of Congress and the Johnson administration.

Although his public discrediting of the Shah infuriated certain elements of the US State Department (which believed the Shah was an essential pillar of US interests in the Persian Gulf), it undoubtably also had the blessing, if not the backing, of some elements within government and intelligence circles.

There's certainly evidence that Khan was doing something that the British and US governments perceived as worthwhile. In

London, two Scotland Yard detectives provided security for him, and he drove a Rolls Royce with Washington DC plates. Once in the US, the House of Representatives filed a bill to grant him political and economic relief from the oppression of the Iranian government.

Given Khan's background, political connections and wealth, it's highly unusual that he would choose to serve the Kennedy campaign as a local volunteer. The timing of his volunteer work is also strange. Although he claimed to have "personally spent considerable time" at Kennedy headquarters, in reality he'd only worked there four days (June 1-4).

Of course, none of these oddities render Khan guilty of anything. But the question remains why the investigating agencies simply ignored Khan's background as a master of espionage. Was it simply to avoid acknowledging Khan's sightings of the woman in the polka-dot dress? Or was it because Khan might alert the LAPD to conspiratorial leads that they were determined not to pursue?

Chapter 4

Sirhan's motives

Since the evidence for a second gunman wasn't made public by the LAPD or probed at Sirhan's trial, and the roles of possible accomplices were suppressed, the media and the public readily accepted Sirhan's confession of guilt and his professed motive—that he'd killed Bobby Kennedy for political reasons.

On the surface, there's no reason to doubt this—his background, notebook and the newspaper clipping in his pocket on the night of the assassination all seem to show that he was a political assassin. But a closer look at the evidence casts doubt on that conclusion.

First, the political content of Sirhan's notebook is overrated. Although there are anti-American, pro-communist sentiments expressed there, the main theme in the 48 pages of scrawls and scribbles—excluding blank pages and classroom notes from his courses at Pasadena City College (PCC)—is money, not politics. In fact, there are twice as many references to money as to any other subject. In addition, the pro-communist sentiments expressed in the notebook are at odds with Sirhan's life. Walter Crowe, Sirhan's closest friend at PCC, became a communist after transferring to another college. Crowe told the FBI that Sirhan wasn't interested in discussing Marxism or communism with him, and had never joined a communist organization.

Second, Sirhan not only lacked interest in communism but seemed uninterested in politics in general. He was a member of the Organization of Arab Students at Pasadena City College, but this was "a social organization" for Arab students, not a political group. Kanan Hamzek, the head of the organization, told the LAPD that Sirhan was very interested in school work but didn't seem to care about politics. Crowe had once tried to form a Students for a Democratic Society group at the college; Sirhan was "apathetic" and wouldn't participate.

Third, Sirhan didn't profess a political motive when first interrogated by police. Far from being a political fanatic trying to make a statement through a violent act, Sirhan never even gave a reason for his violent assault. He didn't begin to profess a political motive until weeks after his arrest.

Even then, his statement lacked conviction. Eduard Simpson, a San Quentin psychologist who worked extensively with Sirhan in 1969, after his sentencing, described Sirhan's comments about Arab-Israeli politics relating to the assassination as "very repetitious," spoken "like an actor playing a role, reading a script." Simpson felt that Sirhan didn't speak with the hesitancy and rephrasing that are common in genuine expressions of thought and emotion.

Fourth, even if it could be proven that Sirhan was politically motivated to commit murder, that wouldn't explain why he singled out RFK. After all, Democratic presidential candidates Hubert Humphrey and Eugene McCarthy and Republican candidate Richard Nixon were all strong supporters of Israel. So was President Lyndon Johnson, who was certainly in a better position than RFK to directly influence policy towards Israel.

So why did Sirhan shoot at Kennedy? Sirhan's acquaintances couldn't imagine. In the dozens of interviews conducted with virtually everyone known to have had contact with Sirhan in the year before the assassination, the interviewees said Sirhan had *never* commented on Kennedy's support of Israel, on the impact of his possible presidency on Middle East politics, or on anything at all relating RFK to the Jews, the Israelis or the Middle East.

Lacking a strong link between Sirhan and Kennedy, authorities tried to provide their own. The official story is that Sirhan was incensed over recent publicity showing RFK's support for the sale of 50 Phantom jets to Israel. Authorities reasoned that since there'd been a television documentary and radio show in the weeks before the assassination (in which Kennedy was

alleged to have pledged the jets to Israel),
these programs must have been the catalyst for both the May 18 journal entry
about RFK and the subsequent murder.

That view is suspect on many counts.
Neither the documentary nor the radio
show specifically mentioned the jet sale. In
fact, the documentary had nothing more
specific about Middle East politics than the
image of an Israeli flag and an announcer
saying that Kennedy had decided to "play a
role in the affairs of men and nations." And
since the documentary aired on May 20,
and the radio show shortly after that, neither could have been the catalyst for
Sirhan's May 18 journal entry.

It's true that, by the time of the trial,
Sirhan himself linked the jet sale to the
murder. But his linking of these two topics
might have been unintentionally created,
rather than uncovered, in pre-trial hypnotic sessions with defense psychiatrist Dr.
Bernard Diamond. (He'd suggested Sirhan
undergo hypnosis to help him remember
basics about the crime.)

Diamond spent approximately 20 hours
with Sirhan. In some of the hypnotic sessions, Diamond asked Sirhan to visualize
the jet bombers at the same time that he
visualized Kennedy moving toward him and
he reached for his gun. According to Dr.
David Spiegal, one of the country's leading
experts on the uses of hypnosis in law

enforcement, a hypnotic subject can be contaminated by artificially creating or reinforcing impressions that'll seem real but aren't. After hypnosis, the subject will mistake the hypnotic experience for a true memory. So it's possible that Sirhan was inadvertently hypno-programmed to connect RFK, the jets and the shooting.

Fifth, although Sirhan continues to support the official view today, his position can be explained by the politics of parole. Since the jury that convicted him in 1969 judged him sane at the time of the crime, Sirhan must acknowledge his guilt and express remorse in order to be paroled. The best way to do that is to take the official view— that he was a political fanatic—and express regret that he acted upon his beliefs. If he were to speak out now about a clouded memory or muddled motive, it would only hurt his chance for freedom.

It's clear that the question of Sirhan's motive is more complicated than it was made to appear by the LA authorities or the media. To say that Sirhan shot RFK for political reasons asks us to believe something quite improbable—that Sirhan, a man without any history of violent acts, political fanaticism or interest in the impact of RFK's candidacy on the Middle East, suddenly became so obsessed with RFK's support of Israel that he committed murder.

Hypnotic programming

If Sirhan wasn't politically motivated, then why did he kill RFK? Although it's divorced from everyday experience, the most plausible explanation is that he was *programmed* to do it.

Sirhan's behavior the night of the assassination provides clues that this might be the case. At 10 pm, Carrilo Cetina, a waiter at the Ambassador, exchanged a few words with Sirhan outside the men's room. He didn't notice anything odd about Sirhan's behavior, but approximately a half hour later, Sirhan was behaving very differently. A brief LAPD summary of an interview with Mary Grohs, a teletype operator stationed near the pantry, described Sirhan as "staring fixedly" at the teletype. In a later interview with investigative journalist Robert Kaiser, Grohs reported, "I'll never forget his eyes....He just kept staring."

Then there was Sirhan's eerie smile as he stood waiting in the pantry. Waiter Vincent Di Pierro told the LAPD that when he saw Sirhan standing in the pantry moments before the shooting, what most stood out in his mind was Sirhan's "stupid smile. A very sick-looking smile." Waiter Martin Patruski and busboy Juan Romero also described Sirhan as "smiling" when he approached Kennedy.

Another witness noted that during the shooting Sirhan looked "very tranquil."

Just after the shooting, writer George Plimpton was taken aback by Sirhan's "dark brown and enormously peaceful" eyes. But by the time Sirhan was pinned down on the steam table, he was demonstrating almost fanatical strength. It took Karl Uecker, two burly, world-class athletes (Rosie Grier and Rafer Johnson) and several other people thirty to forty seconds to get Sirhan's gun away, during which time Sirhan still managed to fire six more shots. As Plimpton observed in a decided understatement, "he was very strong for a small man."

Sirhan continued to behave strangely during the first recorded police interview, at about 12:45 am. The audio tapes revealed that Sirhan was very reluctant to talk; when he did, he mumbled rapidly in a hoarse, weak voice. He also drew deep, erratic breaths, gasping for air as if hyperventilating. At one point he asked for a sip of hot chocolate from a police officer's cup. When the officer refused, Sirhan kicked the cup out of his hands, spilling it on the floor.

By the time of the second interview, at 3:15 am, Sirhan had undergone a striking transformation. LAPD's *Summary Report* described him as "relaxed, polite, composed" and "alertly respond[ing]" to questions. The tapes revealed that his voice was stronger and louder, his words well articulated, and his breathing normal. In contrast to his earlier hostility, he now seemed cheery and deferential, even initiating philosophical discussions about law enforcement with a sense of humor. (The LAPD tried to downplay the change in Sirhan's behavior. Sergeant William Jordan, for example, called it a "slight" change.)

These behavioral changes could have been caused by alcohol or drugs (Sirhan drank three Tom Collinses early in the evening). We'll never know what chemicals might have been influencing Sirhan, because police didn't test him for them— only for syphilis!

But even if Sirhan was under the influence of a drug, that alone wouldn't explain some of the most bizarre aspects about the case. Why can't he remember writing the scribbles in his notebook (or understand what some of the entries refer to), even under hypnosis? And why doesn't he remember anything about the crucial events on the evening of June 4, when he planned and executed the shooting? The hypothesis that he was programmed best accounts for all these facts.

Three theories have been put forward about how this programming might have occurred. One, by defense psychiatrist Bernard Diamond, is that Sirhan programmed himself to kill Kennedy. There's some support for this view from Sirhan's life. In September 1967, Sirhan had fallen off a horse. His injuries weren't serious, but he was plagued by blurred vision and pain, and had to give up his lifelong dream of becoming a jockey. The fall also caused noticeable changes in his behavior. Before the accident he'd been polite and talkative; afterwards Sirhan's brother described him as "withdrawn" and "irritable."

During this period, Sirhan consulted numerous doctors to try and alleviate his symptoms. He also became fascinated by topics like self-hypnosis, mind control and mysticism. We don't know everything he might have tried, because he dropped out of sight between January and March 1968, but we do know that he joined the Rosicrucians, an organization that reinforced his own interest in the occult and in mysticism.

Diamond reasoned that Sirhan had learned to hypnotize himself during this period, even to the point of subconsciously reinforcing, if not creating, a desire to kill Kennedy. But, according to hypnotherapist Dr. John Walters, the problem with this theory is that "you can get yourself into a hypnotic state...but when you start giving yourself a suggestion, it's back at a conscious level again." So it would be almost impossible to program oneself to commit an act without remembering it, especially an act contrary to one's usual behavior (and Sirhan had no history of violent behavior).

Journalist Robert Blair Kaiser (who was a member of Sirhan's defense team and directly observed Sirhan's post-crime hypnotic sessions and discussions with defense lawyers) has a second theory about Sirhan's programming. In a 1970 interview with the *Chicago Tribune,* he flatly stated what his book, *"RFK Must Die!",* only hinted at: "Sirhan was programmed to kill Bob Kennedy and was programmed to forget the fact of his programming." Kaiser refused to name whom he thought did the programming, but his book seemed to suggest it was someone involved with the Rosicrucians, or perhaps a friend of Sirhan's interested in mind control.

Kaiser also theorized that a Rosicrucian article entitled "Write It Down" might have been the catalyst for the repetitive writing in Sirhan's notebook. (Some experts, on the other hand, believed this was a form of "automatic writing"—using repetitive, subconscious writing to create or reinforce ideas.)

There are several problems with Kaiser's theory. First, it seems to imply that the Rosicrucians were experienced hypnotists, but that's not the case. Neither their literature nor the organization itself taught hypnosis or self-hypnosis—only mysticism and positive thinking.

Second, it's doubtful that the Rosicrucian article was the catalyst behind Sirhan's notebook, because the article was merely about using writing to reinforce positive thinking. It claimed, for example, that "writing it down brings it into focus, clarifies it, makes you pin down exactly what you wish to achieve." In other words, the goal was to increase one's conscious awareness of the idea, not to attempt to bypass the conscious mind (which is what happened in Sirhan's case).

Third, it's highly unlikely a friend or acquaintance would've had the expertise to both create a programmed killer and to write himself out of that killer's mind, leaving no clues about who'd done the programming. According to experienced hypnotists, that requires highly sophisticated skills.

This leaves a third option, advocated by William Turner and Jonn Christian in their 1978 book *The Assassination of Robert F. Kennedy.* They say Sirhan was programmed by an expert or experts working for, or in the shadow of, US intelligence.

Because of the sensational nature of this "Manchurian Candidate" theory, it has been misunderstood and largely rejected by scholars, journalists and even hypnotherapists. *(The Manchurian Candidate* is a 1962 movie about a man programmed to assassinate a presidential candidate.) Dr. Robert Fields, a prominent hypnotherapist in Los Angeles, speaks for many when he says, "You simply cannot go beyond what the subject is willing to do....You cannot control people for long periods of time and require them to forget, while still having them function."

But a great deal of solid evidence and expert opinion says that it *is* possible to create a hypno-programmed assassin, given the right conditions. Dr. Milton Kline, a New York psychologist who once served as president of the American Society for Clinical and Experimental Hypnosis, says, "It cannot be done by everyone. It cannot be done consistently, but it can be done." He estimated that he could create a programmed assassin in six months.

Dr. Herbert Spiegal agreed: "It is by no means simple, but under the right circumstances it is definitely attainable." Successfully programming an assassin would depend upon the susceptibility of the subject, the skill and ruthlessness of the programmer, the amount of access to the subject, and the circumstances of access.

Since World War II, the US military and the CIA have conducted extensive research into mind control and its relation to national security. It began when the American military discovered, through captured files, that the Nazis had been conducting mind-control experiments with drugs and hypnosis. Although it seemed the Nazis had never managed to actually gain control of their subjects' minds, the

US military immediately began to question whether the Soviets might succeed—or possibly had already succeeded—where the Nazis had failed.

Fearing that the Russians might produce a "sleeper killer" as a weapon against the West, the CIA began to pursue research on their own programmed assassin. An agency memo in January 1954 discussed a "hypothetical problem": "Can an individual...be made to perform an act of attempted assassination involuntarily?" Can someone be turned into a "trigger mechanism" that can be "induced to perform the act of attempted assassination at a later date"? The target of the attempted assassination was to be "a prominent politician [of the foreign country] or *if necessary an American official*" (my emphasis).

A variation of Turner and Christian's theory is that Sirhan was programmed as a patsy. In *The Search for the Manchurian Candidate,* John Marks quotes an unidentified veteran CIA researcher who says that it would be much easier to create a "patsy," programmed to "make authorities think the patsy committed a particular crime," than to program a robot assassin. Hypnosis expert Milton Kline, who served as an unpaid consultant to CIA researchers, estimated that he could create a patsy in three months.

The CIA has steadfastly maintained that the Manchurian Candidate program was never put into practice. But even if this is true (and there's no reason to believe it is), it doesn't mean that an assassin couldn't have been created by a rogue element of the CIA or someone affiliated, or formerly affiliated, with CIA research. Since mind-control research was conducted at an unknown number of hospitals, private clinics and institutes, and by a diverse group of academics, stage hypnotists and clinical practitioners, it couldn't be strictly controlled. As one source familiar with CIA researchers put it, the agency "approached a lot of the wrong people" in its efforts to understand and practice this type of hypnotic control.

Defense psychiatrist Diamond found that Sirhan could be hypnotized extremely quickly, simply by having him look at a coin; he didn't require protracted suggestions of sleepiness or mesmerizing motions. After reading transcripts and listening to tapes of Sirhan's sessions with Diamond, Dr. Herbert Spiegal concluded that Sirhan was a "grade five," the best type of hypnotic subject. "Less than ten percent of the population rates a grade five," Spiegal says.

A susceptible subject like Sirhan could be programmed to commit a crime without knowing he was doing it, while at the same time appearing to have criminal intent, in order to direct attention away from his programmer. And Sirhan himself could also be turned into the best propagandist for the lone-gun theory, because once subjects undergo skilled programming, they become highly defensive about anything that challenges what the programmers want them to believe.

Sirhan continued to insist that he was a lone assassin, despite having no way of knowing that for sure and even when evidence to the contrary might have helped him in court. He accepted the chance of being sentenced to the gas chamber rather than exploring the possibility that someone may have tampered with his mind. He still hasn't changed his story.

Who programmed Sirhan?

Although, needless to say, no one knows who Sirhan's programmer might have been, Turner and Christian's book points to a likely candiate—the late Dr. William Joseph Bryan Jr., a hypnosis superstar.

Bryan became famous when some of the nation's top lawyers enlisted his help with their cases. Los Angeles attorney Henry Rothblatt described him as "the most brilliant man in the field of hypnotism," as well as the "most knowledgeable and imaginative....There is nothing he hasn't experimented with."

F. Lee Bailey had Bryan study the background of two accused murderers to determine the source of their rage. In the case of the "Hollywood Strangler," Harvey Bush,

Bryan decided that Bush's hatred for his mother had motivated the killings. When Bryan hypnotized Bush in his cell and cast his attorney in the role of Bush mother, Bush violently attacked the attorney.

Bryan also hypnotized the "Boston Strangler," Albert DiSalvo. When Bryan repeatedly suggested that DiSalvo had been symbolically murdering his daughter, who'd diverted his wife's affection from him, DiSalvo's hands lurched up from his lap and grabbed Bryan's throat. Bryan had to yell "sleep!" to protect himself.

Turner and Christian's suspicion that Bryan programmed Sirhan stemmed from some intriguing tidbits of circumstantial data, which has since been expanded upon by the work of other investigators. Two prostitutes who claimed to have serviced Bryan regularly told Christian that Bryan indulged his enormous ego by bragging about his most famous cases, including those of DiSalvo and Sirhan. The women thought nothing about mentioning Bryan's comments about Sirhan, because they thought Bryan had been called in by law-enforcement authorities after Sirhan's arrest.

Turner and Christian also asserted that within hours of Kennedy's assassination, before Sirhan's identity was known, Bryan made an interesting comment while being interviewed on KABC radio in Los Angeles. The show wasn't about the assassination, but the subject briefly came up. Bryan offhandedly suggested that RFK's assailant may have been acting under "post-hypnotic suggestion."

A third link that Turner and Christian uncovered was a reference to DiSalvo in Sirhan's notebook—"God help me, please help me. Salvo Di De Salvo Die S Salvo." When they asked Sirhan about it, he claimed it was completely foreign to him. (It's likely Sirhan was telling the truth, because just hours after the shooting, Sirhan's idle chatter with a jailer, Mr. Foster, was captured on tape. Foster told Sirhan about a book he'd been reading on the Boston Strangler. Sirhan at first couldn't recall the story. When he thought he remembered the case, he guessed that it had happened within the last year, not in 1962 or 1963, as Foster claimed.) It's possible that Sirhan wrote the journal entry because Bryan bragged about the case while programming Sirhan and inadvertently instilled the name in his mind.

One of Bryan's colleagues claimed Bryan had admitted working for the CIA and that he seemed familiar with the idea of creating a robot assassin. This same colleague had also heard through the professional grapevine that Bryan was the technical consultant for the film *The Manchurian Candidate*.

Bryan died in 1977, apparently from natural causes. We may never know for sure if he was Sirhan's programmer, but it's possible that top-notch hypnotist Jonathan Reisner (a pseudonym to protect his identity) might also know something about the case.

When one hypnosis expert was shown examples of the released CIA documents on hypnosis, his first comment was that it read like a textbook written by Reisner. This same source, who also knew Bryan, said that while Bryan was definitely connected to the CIA, Reisner also "could very well have been." He referred to a gap in Reisner's career, which he speculated might have been spent in intensive federal service.

When I interviewed Reisner in 1987, he stated that the idea of a robot assassin was preposterous. He claimed that he knew Bryan "very well" but had never worked with him. And yet, later in the interview, he mentioned having been a technical advisor for *The Manchurian Candidate,* the film on which Bryan allegedly also worked.

In all of this, one thing seems clear: if Sirhan was programmed, it's likely that the CIA, or someone then or formerly connected with it, must have been involved; the CIA had unique expertise to create a programmed assassin.

Chapter Five

Who had a motive?

Who hated Bobby Kennedy enough to have him murdered? RFK began to accrue enemies during his brother's presidency (when he served as attorney general). Both Kennedys angered some of the most powerful individuals or groups in America, including:

- the Mafia, who'd been the victim of the administration's unprecedented crackdown on organized crime (RFK had actually deported New Orleans Mafia boss Carlos Marcello)

- FBI director J. Edgar Hoover, who'd been forced by the attorney general to go after the Mafia (Hoover had denied for years that organized crime existed and preferred to concentrate on eliminating "communists")

- elements of the CIA, who'd participated in the 1961 attempt to overthrow Fidel Castro at the Bay of Pigs (the Kennedy brothers—who felt they'd been misled by the CIA about the strength of Castro's forces—refused to send air support when the invaders met powerful resistance; afterwards, JFK fired CIA director Allen Dulles, and Bobby Kennedy took on a role in CIA policy that was anathema to some of the most swashbuckling CIA veterans)

The old animosities only increased when RFK announced his candidacy for the Democratic nomination. Both his old enemies and several new ones had a lot to lose from an RFK presidency. That list included:

- ex-Teamsters boss Jimmy Hoffa, whom RFK, as attorney general, had sent to prison for jury tampering (if RFK became president, Hoffa would have had to serve his entire thirteen year sentence, but President Nixon pardoned him)

- right-wing and racist groups, like the Ku Klux Klan, who feared RFK's strong commitment to civil rights

- Southern California ranchers who feared Kennedy's support of César Chávez and the United Farm Workers Union—and who, according to an FBI report, had once put out a $500,000 contract on RFK's life (if the union leaders succeeded in organizing thousands of farm workers, the ranchers' profits and power would plummet)

- hard-line cold warriors in the military and intelligence community—even the defense industry—who saw that an RFK presidency would create a complete reversal of US policy in Vietnam

With enemies like these, the pat explanation that Sirhan Sirhan assassinated RFK for his support of Israel seems far less persuasive—especially since RFK's Middle East stance differed very little from the other candidates'. The individuals or groups mentioned above had much more powerful reasons to keep RFK from becoming president in 1968.

Chapter 6

Re-opening the case

The question is often asked: why bother to re-investigate this case? It's been so long— why stir up painful memories?

There are at least three arguments for re-investigation. First, and most obviously, if Sirhan didn't kill RFK, his murderers should be brought to justice.

Second, we need to understand the root causes of the violence that threatens our democratic system. It's important to know whether Robert Kennedy was killed because of a muddled young Palestinian with a political grudge, or because powerful interests in America didn't want him to be president. If the latter's the case, those powerful interests can strike again, whenever they feel threatened.

Third, the LAPD's handling of the case must be reviewed, because law enforcement agencies and officials must be accountable to the public. The JFK and MLK assassinations have both been reviewed by organizations beyond the local jurisdiction, but the RFK assassination case has never been.

What should be done

The best solution would be to appoint a special prosecutor or an independent commission, with subpoena power and investigative resources. This prosecutor or committee should try to:

- establish the location of the extra bullets, in order to provide clues to the position and possible identity of a second gunman
- use sophisticated techniques unavailable in 1968 to simulate bullet trajectories and to analyze and enhance photographic evidence
- question witnesses in depth about the woman in the polka-dot dress
- deprogram Sirhan's mind
- pursue the avenues of investigation covered up or ignored by the LAPD—avenues that still exist after 25 years

Even if it's too late to bring RFK's murderers to justice, it will strengthen American democracy to know the truth about his murder. That truth can help check the powerful interests who manipulate the American political process to their own ends.

How you can help

- Write Los Angeles Mayor Tom Bradley, Room 305, City Hall, 200 N Spring St, Los Angeles CA 90012. Urge him to facilitate an investigation outside the jurisdiction of the LAPD or LADA.

- Write your elected representatives, asking them to seek a federal probe of the case. All the address you need is their names and the following: US House of Representatives, Washington DC 20515 or US Senate, Washington DC 20510.

- Keep informed about the case by contacting the Inquiry and Accountability Foundation, a nonprofit, tax-exempt organization that's attempting to re-open the case, and which provides information to the public and media. It's at Box 85065, Los Angeles CA 90027. Even better, support their work.

Recommended reading

Kaiser, Robert Blair. *"RFK Must Die!"* Grove Press, 1970.

Melanson, Philip. *The Robert F. Kennedy Assassination.* Shapolsky, 1991.

Newfield, Jack. *Robert Kennedy: a Memoir.* Bantam Books, 1969.

Turner, William and Jonn Christian. *The Assassination of Robert F. Kennedy: a Conspiracy and Cover-Up.* Thunder's Mouth Press, 1993.

Notes

Most of the material for this book comes from LAPD and FBI files that were released in the late 1980s, and from the author's interviews with witnesses and investigators. Other sources are listed below by page numbers and brief subject descriptions. Full publication data is given the first time a work is cited (except for the books listed on the previous page, whose names are bolded the first time they're cited below.)

Chapter 1

5. Effects of Johnson's re-election. *US News and World Report,* 5/6/68, p. 54.

6. RFK's campaign speech.*Life,* Jun 88, p. 38.

11. Sirhan's memory. **Kaiser,** pp. 304, 350–51, 366, 368.

11–12. Sirhan's background. James W. Clarke, *American Assassins.* Princeton University Press, 1982, pp. 79–85.

14. Sirhan's trial. *People of the State of California v. Sirhan Bishara Sirhan,* 1969, Superior Court Criminal Case #14062.

Chapter 2

28. Warren Commission's magic bullet. See Carl Oglesby, *Who Killed JFK?* Odonian Press, pp. 18, 27–29, 30–32, 54–55 for more details.

30–31. Bugliosi affidavits. **Turner and Christian,** pp. 179–81, appendix.

37. Mysterious deaths of JFK witnesses. See Carl Oglesby, *Who Killed JFK?* Odonian Press, pp. 71–74 for more details.

38–39. LAPD's response to Schulman. Carolyn M. Smith. "Don Schulman: A Key Witness," paper presented in Political Science 444, University of Massachusetts, Dartmouth, Fall 1988.

39. Cesar's employment at Ace Guard. Dan E. Moldea, "Who Really Killed Bobby Kennedy?" *Regardies,* Jun 87, p. 74.

40.   Cesar's proximity to RFK. Ted Charach, *The Second Gun,* 1971.

42.   Cesar's right-wing views. See Charach.

42.   Cesar's hatred of the Kennedys. Moldea, p. 73.

42.   Cesar's mob contacts. Discussed in David Sheim, *Contract on America,* Shapolsky, 1988, p. 294.

42–43. Cesar hasn't prospered since the murder. Moldea, p. 77.

Chapter 3

52.   Schraga encounters the Bernsteins. Interview with Jack Thomas, KUOP Radio, Modesto CA, 5/18/88.

53–54. Schraga's APB. See William Turner and Jonn Christian, "California Assassination Archives—Robert F. Kennedy," and "Polka-Dots and Police Perfidy," *Easy Reader,* 11/17/88.

61.   LAPD's information on Khan. LAPD *Summary Report* of investigation into the Robert F. Kennedy assassination, pp. 425–39.

61–63. Khan's background. Fred J. Cook, "The Billion-Dollar Mystery," *The Nation,* 4/12/65, pp. 380–97.

Chapter 4

64–65. Crowe becomes a communist. *Summary Report,* pp. 69–72 at p. 71.

65.   Sirhan's interest in politics. Kaiser, pp. 111–13, 163–65.

65–66. Simpson's testimony. Taped interview with Betsy Langman, 1974.

69.   Cetina's testimony. LAPD interview, 9/11/68.

69.   Grohs' testimony. Kaiser, pp. 531–32.

69.   Sirhan's smile. Kaiser, p. 26.

69–70. Sirhan's tranquility. Turner and Christian, p. 197; Plimpton's 6/5/68 LAPD interview (audio tape).

70.   Time to get Sirhan's gun away. This comes from an audio-taped description of the struggle narrated by Andrew West of Mutual News Radio.

70–71. Sirhan's transformation. *Summary Report,* p. 625.

71. Sirhan didn't recognize his writing. Kaiser, pp. 339–40, 264–65.

72. Sirhan's fall. Kaiser, pp. 207–8.

72. Sirhan's change in behavior. Kaiser, pp. 133–34.

72. Sirhan drops out of sight. Turner and Christian, p. 224.

72. John Walters. Langman, 1974.

73. Rosicrucians didn't teach hypnosis. Pamela Puputti, "Did the Rosicrucians Influence the Behavior of Sirhan Sirhan to Participate in the Assassination of Robert F. Kennedy?" University of Massachusetts, Dartmouth, Seminar on Political Assassination, Fall 1988.

73–74. Rosicrucian article. "Write It Down," *Rosicrucian Digest,* excerpts read into trial transcript, pp. 4975–76.

75. Milton Kline. John D. Marks, *The Search for the "Manchurian Candidate,"* McGraw-Hill, 1980, p. 182, note on p. 190.

76. CIA memo. Marks, p. 31.

76. Programming a patsy. Marks, p. 191.

78. Sirhan defends lone-gun theory. Taped interviews of Dr. Eduard Simpson and Dr. Martin Schorr with Betsy Langman, 1974.

78. Rothblatt praises Bryan. Langman, 1974.

78–79. Bryan's hypnotizes the Boston Strangler. F. Lee Bailey with Harvey Aronson, *The Defense Never Rests,* Stein and Day, 1971, pp. 159–61, 165.

79. Bryan's prostitutes. Turner and Christian, p. 228.

79–80. Bryan's radio interview. Turner and Christian, p. 226.

80. Sirhan's DiSalvo reference. Turner and Christian, p. 227.

80. Bryan's work on *Manchurian Candidate.* Turner and Christian, p. 206.

Index

More books in the Real Story series
(see the next page for other titles)

Who Killed Martin Luther King?
Philip Melanson
This fascinating investigation of a murder that changed history shows why the official story just doesn't make sense.

Who Killed JFK?   Carl Oglesby
This brief but fact-filled book gives you the inside story on the most famous crime of the century. You won't be able to put it down.

Burma: The Next Killing Fields?
Alan Clements
If we don't do something about Burma, it will become another Cambodia. Written by one of the few Westerners ever to have lived there, this book tells the story vividly.

Real Story books are available at most good bookstores, or send $5 per book + $2 shipping *per order* (not per book) to Odonian Press, Box 7776, Berkeley CA 94707. Please write for information on quantity discounts, or call us at 800 REAL STORY or 510 524 4000.

*The Real Story series
is based on a simple idea—
political books don't have to be boring.
Short, well-written and to the point,
Real Story books are meant to be <u>read</u>.*

*If you liked this book,
check out some of our others:*

The Prosperous Few and the Restless Many
Noam Chomsky

A wide-ranging state-of-the-world report by the man the *New York Times* calls "arguably the most important intellectual alive."   *Fall, 1993*

The Greenpeace Guide to Anti-
environmental Organizations   Carl Deal

This comprehensive guide describes dozens of industry front groups that masquerade as environmental organizations.

The Decline and Fall of the American Empire
Gore Vidal

Vidal is one of our most important—and wittiest—social critics. This little book is the perfect introduction to his political views.

What Uncle Sam Really Wants
Noam Chomsky

A brilliant analysis of the real motivations behind US foreign policy, from one of America's most popular speakers. Full of astounding information.

For ordering information, see the preceding page.